W. W. Jacobs'

The Monkey's Paw

Peter Leigh

Published in association with The Basic Skills Agency

Hodder & Stoughton

A MEMBER OF THE HODDER HEADLINE

D1393359

Acknowledgements
Cover: Dave Smith
Illustrations: Linda Clark
Photograph: Mary Evans Picture Library

Copyright © 2000 The Estate of W.W. Jacobs

Every effort has been made to trace copyright holders of material reproduced in this book. Any rights not acknowledged will be acknowledged in subsequent printings if notice is given to the publisher.

Orders; please contact Bookpoint Ltd, 39 Milton Park, Abingdon, Oxon OX14 4TD. Telephone: (44) 01235 400414, Fax: (44) 01235 400454. Lines are open from 9.00–6.00, Monday to Saturday, with a 24 hour message answering service.
Email address: orders@bookpoint.co.uk

British Library Cataloguing in Publication Data
A catalogue record for this title is available from the British Library

ISBN 0 340 77462 2

First published 2000
Impression number 10 9 8 7 6 5 4 3 2 1
Year   2005 2004 2003 2002 2001 2000

Typeset by GreenGate Publishing Services, Tonbridge, Kent.
Printed in Great Britain for Hodder and Stoughton Educational, a division of Hodder Headline Plc, 338 Euston Road, London NW1 3BH, by Redwood Books, Trowbridge, Wilts

About the author

W.W. Jacobs was born in 1863,
and died in 1943.

He wrote hundreds of stories.
Some of them are very funny.
The most popular one
is this chilling ghost story.

About the Story

It is a wild and wet night.
Inside the little cottage
the curtains are drawn
and the fire is burning brightly.

Mr and Mrs White live there
with their son Herbert.
They are waiting for a visitor.
Father and son are playing chess
to pass the time.

I

hark – listen to

'Hark at the wind,' said Mr White.
He had just made a bad mistake,
and wanted to put Herbert off.

'I'm listening,' said Herbert.
He stretched out his hand.
'Check –'

'I don't think that he'll come tonight,'
said Mr White.

'– mate!' said Herbert.

'That's the worst of living so far out,'
said Mr White angrily.
'Nobody comes to see you.'

'Never mind, dear,' said his wife.
'Perhaps you'll win the next one.'

He knows he is
being made fun of.

Mr White looked up sharply.
He saw a knowing glance
between mother and son.
He grinned to himself.

'There he is,' said Herbert.
The gate banged loudly,
and heavy footsteps
came towards the door.

The old man got up,
and opened the door.

He welcomed in a big, tall man
with a red face.

'This is Sergeant-Major Morris,' he said.

The sergeant-major shook hands,
and was given the seat by the fire.
He watched contentedly
as the old man got out the whisky.

At the third glass his eyes got brighter,
and he began to talk.
The little family circle listened eagerly.
He told them of distant parts,
of wild scenes and brave deeds,
of wars and plagues and strange peoples.

'Twenty-one years of it,'
said Mr White to his wife and son.
'When he went away
he was a slip of a boy.
Now look at him.'

He looks fine.

'He don't look to have taken much harm,'
said Mrs White politely.

'I'd like to go to India myself,'
said the old man.
'Just to look round a bit, you know.'

'Better where you are,'
said the sergeant-major,
shaking his head.
He put down his empty glass,
and sighed softly.

'I should like to see
those old temples and fakirs and jugglers,'
said the old man.
'What was that
you started telling me the other day?
About a monkey's paw or something?'

'Nothing,' said the soldier, hastily.
'At least nothing worth hearing.'

'Monkey's paw?' said Mrs White.
She was curious.

'Well, it's just a bit
of what you might call magic,'
said the sergeant-major.
He tried to sound offhand.

His three listeners
leaned forward eagerly.
The visitor put his empty glass to his lips
and then set it down again.
The old man filled it for him.

'To look at,' said the sergeant-major,
'it's just an ordinary little paw,
dried up now.'

He took something out of his pocket,
and held it up.

Mrs White drew back with a grimace,
but Herbert looked at it curiously.

Mr White took it,
examined it carefully,
and put it on the table.

'And what is there special about it?'
he said.

'An old fakir put a spell on it,'
said the sergeant major.
'He was a very holy man.
He thought that if you interfered with fate
you did so to your own cost.
He put a spell on it
so that three people
can each have three wishes from it.'

The others laughed,
but he was serious.

'Well, why don't you have three?'
said Herbert.

The old soldier looked at the young man.
'I have,' he said quietly,
and his face went pale.

'And were they granted?'
asked Mrs White.

'They were,' he said.

'And has anybody else wished?'
persisted the old lady.

persisted – kept on

'Yes! The first man had his three wishes.
I don't know what the first two were,
but the third was for death.
That's how I got the paw.'

His tones were so grave
that a hush fell upon the group.

5

'If you've had your three wishes,
it's no good to you now,'
said the old man at last.
'What do you keep it for?'

The soldier shook his head.
'Fancy, I suppose,' he said, slowly.
'I did have some idea of selling it,
but I don't think I will.
It has caused enough mischief already.
Besides, people won't buy.
They think it's a fairy tale.
Or they want to try it first
and pay me afterwards.'

'If you could have another three wishes,'
said the old man,
'would you have them?'

'I don't know,' said the other.
'I don't know.'

He took the paw,
and suddenly threw it on the fire.
Mr White, with a slight cry,
stooped down and snatched it off.

'Better let it burn,' said the soldier.

'If you don't want it,
give it to me,' said Mr White.

'I won't!
I threw it on the fire.
If you keep it,
don't blame me for what happens.
Throw it on the fire again
like a sensible man.'

He doesn't really know why he keeps it.

Mr White shook his head.
The paw was his now.
He looked at it closely.
'How do you do it?' he asked.

'Hold it up in your right hand
and wish aloud,'
said the sergeant-major,
'but I warn you of what might happen.'

The Arabian Nights
– a collection of
wonderful stories of
magic from Arabia

'Sounds like The Arabian Nights,'
said Mrs White.
She rose and began to set the supper.
'You could wish for
four pairs of hands for me.'

Her husband drew the paw from his pocket.
The sergeant-major caught him by the arm.
He looked alarmed.
The other three burst into laughter.

gruff – curt and
angry

'If you must wish,' he said, gruffly,
'wish for something sensible.'

enthralled – they
are completely
captured by his
stories

Mr White dropped it back in his pocket.
He set the chairs,
and they sat down at the table.
Over supper the paw was forgotten.
Afterwards the three listened enthralled
to some more stories
of the soldier's adventures in India.

After he left Herbert said,
'If the tale about the monkey's paw
is as true as the others,
then we shan't make much out of it.'

'Did you give him anything for it?'
asked Mrs White,
looking at her husband closely.

'A little,' said he.
He blushed slightly.
'He didn't want it,
but I made him take it.
And he told me again to throw it away.'

'Very likely,' said Herbert.
'Why, we're going to be rich,
and famous and happy.
Wish to be a king to begin with, father.
Then you can't be henpecked!'

henpecked –
nagged

He darted round the table,
chased by Mrs White.

Mr White took the paw from his pocket.
He eyed it doubtfully.
'I don't know what to wish for,
and that's a fact,' he said slowly.
'It seems to me I've got all I want.'

'If you could just pay for the house,
you'd be happy, wouldn't you?'
said Herbert,
with his hand on his shoulder.
When this story was
written £200 was
worth a lot more than
it is today.

'Well, wish for two hundred pounds then;
that'll just do it.'

8

His father smiled a little.
He thought it was silly.
He held up the paw,
and said clearly,
'I wish for two hundred pounds.'

Suddenly he cried out loud,
and dropped the paw.
His wife and son ran towards him.

'It moved,' he said.
'As I wished,
it twisted in my hand like a snake.'
He looked at the paw as it lay on the floor
with a glance of disgust.

'Well, I don't see the money,'
said Herbert.
He picked up the paw,
and placed it on the table.
'And I bet I never shall.'

'It must have been your imagination,'
said Mrs White.
She looked at her husband anxiously.

He shook his head.
'Never mind, though.
There's no harm done,
but it gave me a shock all the same.'

They sat down by the fire again.
Outside the wind was higher than ever.
The old man started nervously
as a door banged upstairs.
All three were silent.
At last the old couple got up
to go to bed.

started – jumped
nervously

'I expect you'll find the cash
tied up in a big bag
in the middle of your bed,'
said Herbert, as he said goodnight.

After they had gone to bed,
he sat alone in the darkness.
He gazed at the dying fire,
seeing faces in it.

The last face was horrible
and like a monkey.
It got so vivid that,
with a little uneasy laugh,
he felt on the table for a glass of water
to throw over it.
His hand grasped the monkey's paw.
With a little shiver
he wiped his hand on his coat,
and went up to bed.

II

At breakfast next morning,
Herbert laughed at his fears
from the night before.

'I suppose all old soldiers are the same,'
said Mrs White.
'The idea of us listening to such nonsense!
How could wishes be granted in these days?
And if they could,
how could two hundred pounds hurt you,
father?'

'Might drop on his head from the sky,'
said Herbert jokingly.

'He said the things happened so naturally,'
said his father,
'that you could think it chance.'

'Well, don't break into the money
before I come back,'
said Herbert as he got up from the table.
'It'll turn you into a miser,
and we shall have to disown you.'

His mother laughed,
as she followed him to the door.
She watched him fondly down the road.

miser – someone who is very mean with money
disown you – push you out of the family

Later that day,
as she sat with her husband at dinner,
she said,
'I expect Herbert
will have some more of his jokes,
when he comes home.'

'I dare say,' said Mr White.
'But for all that,
the thing moved in my hand.
That I'll swear to.'

'You thought it did,'
said the old lady soothingly.

'I say it did,' replied the other.
'There was no thought about it.
I had just – What's the matter?'

His wife made no reply.
She was watching a man outside.
He was acting strangely.
He looked as if he was trying
to make up his mind to come in.

Three times he stopped at the gate,
and then walked on again.
The fourth time
he stood with his hand upon it.
Then suddenly he flung it open,
and walked up the path.

Mrs White went to the door,
and brought the stranger into the room.
He was well-dressed,
but he seemed ill at ease.

He looked at her,
and then looked away again.
She apologized for the state of the room,
and for her husband's old coat.
Then she waited
for him to state his business.
But he was strangely silent.

At last he said, 'I – was asked to call.
I come from Maw and Meggins.'

The old lady started.
'Is anything the matter?'
she asked, breathlessly.
'Has anything happened to Herbert?
What is it? What is it?'

'There, there, mother,'
said her husband, hastily.
'Sit down, and don't jump to conclusions.
You've not brought bad news,
I'm sure, sir.'

'I'm sorry –' began the visitor.

'Is he hurt?'
demanded the mother, wildly.

The visitor nodded.
'Badly hurt,' he said, quietly.
'But he is not in any pain.'

'Oh, thank God!' said the old woman,
clasping her hands.
'Thank God for that! Thank –'

She broke off suddenly
as the awful meaning of his words
dawned upon her.
She looked at his face.
He turned away,
and she knew she was right.

She caught her breath,
and turning to her husband,
laid her trembling old hand upon his.
There was a long silence.

'He was caught in the machinery,'
said the visitor in a low voice.

'Caught in the machinery?'
repeated Mr White.

He sat staring blankly out at the window.
He took his wife's hand in his own,
and pressed it as he used to do
in their old courting days
nearly forty years before.

'He was the only one left to us,' he said,
turning gently to the visitor.
'It is hard.'

She realises that
Herbert is dead.

Courting days – in
the early days of
their relaionship,
before they got
married.

The other coughed, and stood up.
He looked out of the window.
'The firm wished me to convey
their sincere sympathy to you
in your great loss.'
He spoke without looking round.

There was no reply.
The old woman's face was white,
her eyes staring.

Liability – blame

'I was to say that
Maw and Meggins
deny any responsibility.
They admit no liability at all,
but because of your son's services,
they wish to present you

compensation – to
make up for it

with a certain sum as compensation.'

Mr White dropped his wife's hand.
He gazed with a look of horror
at his visitor.
His dry lips shaped the words,
'How much?'

'Two hundred pounds!' was the answer.

His wife shrieked.
The old man smiled faintly,
and dropped senseless to the floor.

III

In the huge new cemetery,
some two miles distant,
the old couple buried their son.
They came back to a house
of shadow and silence.

It was all over so quickly
that at first they couldn't realize it.
They were hoping
something else would happen –
something else to lighten this load,
too heavy for old hearts to bear.

resignation –
acceptance

But the days passed,
and hope gave way to resignation –
the hopeless resignation of the old.
Sometimes they hardly said a word,
for now they had nothing to talk about,
and their days were long and weary.

It was about a week after
that the old man woke suddenly
in the night.
He stretched out his hand
and found himself alone.
The room was in darkness.
The sound of quiet weeping
came from the window.

He raised himself in bed and listened.

'Come back,' he said, tenderly.
You will be cold.'

'It is colder for my son,'
said the old woman, and wept afresh.

The sound of her sobs
died away on his ears.
The bed was warm,
and his eyes heavy with sleep.
He dozed fitfully,
until a sudden wild cry from his wife
awoke him with a start.

'The paw!' she cried wildly.
'The monkey's paw!'

He started up in alarm.
'Where? Where is it?
What's the matter?'

She came stumbling across the room
towards him.
'I want it,' she said, quietly.
You've not destroyed it?'

'It's downstairs, on the shelf! Why?'

She cried and laughed together,
and bending over, kissed his cheek.

'I only just thought of it,'
she said hysterically.
'Why didn't I think of it before?
Why didn't you think of it?'

'Think of what?'

'The other two wishes,'
she replied rapidly.
'We've only had one.'

'Was not that enough?'
he demanded, fiercely.

'No,' she cried. 'We'll have one more.
Go down and get it quickly,
and wish our boy alive again.'

The man sat up in bed
and flung off the bedclothes.
'Good God!' he cried.
'You are mad!'

'Get it,' she panted.
'Get it quickly, and wish –
Oh, my boy, my boy!'

Her husband struck a match
and lit the candle.
'Get back to bed,' he said shakily.
'You don't know what you are saying.'

'We had the first wish granted.
Why not the second?'

'A coincidence,'
stammered the old man.

'Go and get it and wish,' cried his wife.
She was quivering with excitement.

The old man turned and looked at her.
His voice shook.
'He has been dead ten days.
And besides he – I didn't tell you this,
but – I could only recognize him
by his clothing.
If he was too terrible
for you to see then,
think what he's like now.'

'Bring him back,' cried the old woman.
She dragged him towards the door.
'Do you think I fear
the child I have nursed?'

He went down in the darkness,
and felt his way to the shelf.
The paw was in its place.
He picked it up,
but a horrible fear seized him,
and he lost the direction of the door.
His brow was cold with sweat.
He felt his way round the table,
and groped along the wall
until he found himself in the hall.

When he got back to the room
even his wife's face seemed changed.
It was white and hopeful.
It seemed to him
to have an unnatural look on it.
He was afraid of her.

'Wish!' she cried, in a strong voice.

falter – hesitate

'It is foolish and wicked,' he faltered.

'Wish!' repeated his wife.

He raised his hand.
'I wish my son alive again.'

The paw fell to the floor,
and he looked at it fearfully.
Then he sank trembling into a chair.
The old woman, with burning eyes,
walked to the window
and opened the curtain.

He sat until he was chilled with the cold.
The old woman stood
staring through the window.
The candle burnt down,
and went out.

The old man was relieved.
The second wish had failed.
He crept back to his bed,
and a minute or two afterwards
the old woman came silently beside him.

Neither spoke,
but lay silently
listening to the ticking of the clock.

A stair creaked,
and a squeaky mouse
scurried along the wall.

After lying for some time
the old man took the box of matches,
and striking one
went downstairs for a candle.

At the foot of the stairs
the match went out,
and he paused to strike another.
At the same moment a knock
sounded on the front door.
It was so quiet and stealthy
that he could hardly hear it.

The matches fell from his hand
and spilled in the passage.

He stood still,
unable to breathe.

The knock was repeated.

He turned,
and fled swiftly back to his room,
and closed the door behind him.
A third knock sounded through the house.

'What's that?'
cried the old woman, starting up.

'A rat!' said the old man in shaking tones.
'A rat. It passed me on the stairs.'

His wife sat up in bed listening.
A loud knock resounded through the house.

'It's Herbert!' she screamed.
'It's Herbert!'

She ran to the door,
but her husband was before her,
and caught her by the arm.
He held her tightly.

'What are you going to do?'
he whispered hoarsely.

'It's my boy, it's Herbert!' she cried.
'I forgot it was two miles away.
What are you holding me for?
Let go. I must open the door.'

'For God's sake don't let it in,'
cried the old man, trembling.

'You're afraid of your own son,' she cried.
'Let me go.
I'm coming, Herbert! I'm coming!'

There was another knock, and another.
The old woman with a sudden wrench
broke free and ran from the room.

Her husband followed to the landing.
He called after her
as she hurried downstairs.

He heard the chain rattle
and the bottom bolt drawn back
slowly and stiffly.

Then the old woman's voice,
strained and panting.
'The top bolt,' she cried, loudly.
'Come down. I can't reach it.'

But her husband was on his hands and knees
groping wildly on the floor.
He was searching for the paw.

If only he could find it
before the thing outside got in!

The knocks hammered through the house now.
He heard the scraping of a chair
as his wife put it down against the door.
He heard the creaking of the bolt
as it came slowly back.
At the same moment
he found the monkey's paw,
and breathed his third and last wish.

The knocking stopped suddenly.
He heard the chair drawn back,
and the door opened.

A cold wind rushed up the staircase.
There was a long loud wail of misery
from his wife.
He ran down to her side,
and then to the gate beyond.
The street lamp opposite
shone on a quiet and deserted road.